D0716004

The
Insider's Guide to
getting a
First
(or avoiding a Third)

PO32532

The
Insider's Guide to
getting a
First

(or avoiding a Third)

Mark Black

Editors: Richard Craze, Roni Jay

new tricks for old dogs

Published by White Ladder Press Ltd
Great Ambrook, Near Ipplepen, Devon TQ12 5UL
01803 813343
www.whiteladderpress.com

First published in Great Britain in 2005

10 9 8 7 6 5 4 3 2

© Mark Black 2005

ISBN 0 9543914 9 7

British Library Cataloguing in Publication Data
A CIP record for this book can be obtained from the British Library.

Designed and typeset by Julie Martin Ltd
Illustrations by Chris Mutter
Cover design by Julie Martin Ltd
Printed and bound by TJ International Ltd, Padstow, Cornwall

The paper used for the text pages of this book is FSC certified.
FSC (The Forest Stewardship Council) is an international network
to promote responsible management of the world's forests.

Printed on totally chlorine-free paper

FSC
Mixed Sources
Product group from well-managed
forests and other controlled sources

Cert no. 908-COC-2482
www.fsc.org
© 1996 Forest Stewardship Council

White Ladder Press
Great Ambrook, Near Ipplepen, Devon TQ12 5UL
01803 813343
www.whiteladderpress.com

Contents

Introduction

This book is a confession of the strategy I used to get a Distinction in my MBA. In case you don't know what that is, an MBA is a Master of Business Administration. A Distinction is the master's level equivalent of a first class honours degree. It means I managed to finish with an average of over 70%.

Getting a First is the dream of many students and most rely on talent to achieve it. I know lots of students who are blessed with the ability to write first class assignment and exam answers off the cuff. There was one man on my course for whom the term blessed is not enough, and he used to write assignments on the day of submission that regularly came back with marks in the high 70s. I, however, am not one of those blessed people. Up to this point I had never produced the goods in an academic sense. That simple fact was a source of great discomfort to me and I was determined to find a way to 'manufacture' this ability that I certainly had not shown throughout my entire academic career.

Throughout school, and my first degree in law, I got *some* good marks. A grades were always welcome, popping up occasionally, but I was never a straight A student and it must be said that English was never my strong point. I never received good marks in English at school and my ability to write a good essay was about as consistent as the lottery numbers. I scraped a 2:2 at law in my degree course, finishing with an average of 52% thanks largely to a heroic effort on my dissertation. Nothing to shout from the rooftops there then, is there?

The challenge

I was faced with a dilemma. I had enrolled on a full time MBA course for one year and had been kindly funded by my parents for a significant sum of money. However, the course would entail writing an awful lot of essays and I was no good at them but really wanted to be. So the dilemma was either come up with something and get good really quickly, or accept that I currently stunk at writing essays and, no matter how good my practical involvement in the course might be, I would not return marks that would do justice to my ambitions, or to the great deal of money that had been invested in me.

I had a certain motivation that forced me into making the first choice. I took my MBA at 22 which, as anyone in the know will realise, is exceptionally young to be taking an MBA. I was nervous. Frightened is probably more accurate if I'm honest. The average age on the course was over 30 and I was significantly younger than most people, except my twin brother Stephen that is, who took the same MBA course. This was to prove a significant advantage; for reasons I'll explain later on.

But back to the point. We were on this course and much younger than anyone else. The MBA is a course that is often about using past experiences to grasp the concepts that are thrown at you at an incredible pace. We had work experience through involvement with running our family company, but we did not have anywhere near the level of experience that the other course members possessed. Less experience is a drawback for this particular course. This put our backs against the wall. No one enjoys looking stupid or naive and no one enjoys not cutting the mustard because they are vastly inexperienced compared to everyone else in the room.

We were facing both in the biggest way. We had to come up with *something* that would at least allow us to hold our own with the other members of the course. Apart from this very powerful personal motivation, we also couldn't ignore the fact that too much money had been invested for us not to make the grade. When I say that, I'm talking about simply passing. When we first started, we were both secretly terrified that we were in way over our heads, and our plan originally came about as a direct result of this fear.

Another factor that played a role was that we were the only British people on our course. That meant 80+ foreigners. This was another intimidation that spurred us on – we were suddenly, if unexpectedly, representing our country. *Do it for England, Mark!* Later, the fact that we were the sole British people on the course was to become a great benefit in our eyes and the connections we have all over the globe are priceless. It's also nice to know that you have friends all around the world. However, that didn't change the initial thoughts we had of, 'Oh my god, what are we up against here?' In our eyes, the university had kindly shipped in business talent from around the world and put them in direct competition with us in some twisted plot to make us look like idiots. 'Bugger' was our first thought.

The start of the plan

And then it came. The moment of inspiration! We stumbled across a proposal that would eventually see us both graduate with Distinctions. The plan was *strategy*. The way I saw it, I couldn't compete on raw talent, because the others had more of it and had proven so over a longer period of time than I had. And I couldn't rely on my essay writing abilities because I didn't have any. The only way I saw that would allow me to hold my own in this lions' den was to have a better strategy for passing the course than anybody else. As the course progressed we suspected that we were on to a good thing with this plan, and towards the end of the first semester I began to suspect we were the only ones with any sort of strategy at all.

The first set of examinations took place in January. After good preparation I was fortunate enough to emerge with the highest average on the course. Stephen followed in hot pursuit in third.

The plan was working. 'Hallelujah!' we thought. The second semester assessments came in the form of assignments for each module. Almost all assessment was essay based and, as luck would have it, drove at the heart of my killer weakness.

This situation posed a slightly different set of challenges and the plan was tweaked accordingly, but the basics remained in place. We followed the strategy with dedication and, after the second semester results came back, I found that I had successfully defended my leading position. Stephen had averaged higher than me in the second semester and we now found ourselves in first and second place. A Distinction was within touching distance for the pair of us.

For our course the dissertation was worth a third of the overall mark. Quite simply, despite all our success in the assessments leading up to the dissertation, without a Distinction in the dissertation we would not achieve a Distinction overall. The strategy did not change from the second semester to the dissertation and we again followed it strictly.

We received our marks on November 5th and were delighted to find that we had both achieved Distinctions in the dissertations, which meant we both came away with Distinctions overall. I had been extremely privileged to have successfully defended my lead a second time, and graduated with the highest average on the course.

This puts me in a unique position. I finished top and successfully achieved a Distinction that was due almost entirely to the strategy that my twin brother and I had formulated and now possessed. Unlike many high achieving students, we had been successful and knew exactly *why*. And we knew why beyond the rather unhelpful comment of 'we just worked hard'. We've all heard the fresher talk: go out and get drunk and you'll get a 2:2, attend more regularly and do a bit and you'll get a 2:1, and to get a First you've got to lock yourself in your room and live in a fashion resembling 15th century monks. That fallacy, I believe, was created to hide the fact that there are ways to get a First or a Distinction by playing the game rather than becoming a recluse.

So there's the background to the strategy and I hope I've at least gone some way towards showing that it works and that it was the reason behind our success. All that I can say is that, at the time of writing, the only two people ever to use it both got Distinctions. How it fares in your hands is up to you. In all honestly I wouldn't divulge the strategy if I thought it would be misleading, and I have a genuine belief that taking this strategy and fitting it in with your own approach will have a positive effect on your marks and certainly improves your chances of gaining a First or a Distinction.

There are ways to get a First or a Distinction by playing the game rather than becoming a recluse.

Avoiding a Third

But remember that this strategy isn't just for those who want a First. It also serves the original purpose of the plan in that it can help struggling students hold their own. Believe me on that one, I've been there and no doubt will probably be there again in the future. It doesn't matter what your ambitions are for your degree; this can make a difference.

I've got to be honest and say that it gives me equal pleasure, if not more, to help someone who's not academically great go from a Fail to a Pass, or from a Third to a 2:1, as it does helping other people get Firsts. That's probably because I've spent a lifetime at the wrong end of the scale and feel more at home there. If anybody had given me a way to stop returning bad marks during my law degree I'd have thought they were an angel.

There are plenty of students who'd be disappointed to get 55%, but when you're constantly sitting with results in your hand that say 38% and 41% then 55% seems a world away. It's only once you've been there that you can truly understand how bad 38% feels. It's like someone walking up and stamping 'useless' on your forehead. I'm pleased to be able to offer a hand to those who are staring straight at a similar position. So without further ado, here is our strategy.

The golden rule is that everything you do must fit with the overall goal of getting a First or a Distinction. Consistency is the key. We tried to show consistency throughout every task, however big or small, so that it was the best that it could be. In almost every case we could say that all aspects of our preparation and work placed us among the best students. If you do the same you stand a very good chance of getting a First, and you'll certainly not fail the course. Only those of us who've been there will understand the relief that comes from knocking that possibility on the head.

Keep it quiet

Something else to mention before we get started is that it's probably best if you don't tell *everyone* that you're following this strategy. Obviously you don't have to treat it like a covert operation, but letting everyone on your course know about your plans gives the game away. As you read through the book you'll come to realise that it's probably in your interest to have a few well chosen people in on the plan. This has a number of advantages that will help you in your efforts, among which are less work and more precise information about what you're trying to do. In particular, don't tell your lecturers. If they get even the slightest inclination that you're trying to work the system it will seriously affect your chances of getting the full benefits that this strategy has to offer.

STRATEGEM

1

Play the Game

An important point is that I didn't see myself as being in education. I saw myself as being in business, with my tutors and lecturers as my bosses. They hold just as much authority over you as a boss would at work and they directly influence your progress just as a normal boss would influence your career progress. If your boss doesn't think you're any good then you aren't going to get promoted. It's the same situation at uni. If your lecturer likes you and thinks that you're someone who wants to make progress, they are far more likely to assist you in this goal.

This may sound blunt but it's true. So run with my logic here and see what you think. The important fact to realise about this 'worker/boss' relationship is that *they* have the authority. They hold all the cards. If and when it comes down to it, their view is right, not yours. The biggest mistake I made when I did my law degree was that I took notice of people who said, "Put your own originality into your answers". To be blunt again, this is bullshit.

If your views do not match the views of the person marking your work then you'll get a poor mark. It doesn't matter that you might be right.

The problem here is that the exams and essays are marked against the textbook answers. But to be *truly* original you've got to say the textbook answers are wrong, which is going to take a lot longer to prove than just doing one piece of coursework. The only way around this is if you argue something that isn't in the textbook. Then you're not stepping on anybody's toes because the textbook doesn't directly say you're mistaken. Even then, it's going to be difficult to get a good mark because there is no authority to support your argument. A good answer always has support so therefore a good answer is never *truly* original.

Mistakes are tempting

I learnt this lesson the hard way many times in law and even made the same mistake on the MBA. That's because, at heart, I'm an idiot. I just love making the same mistakes over and over again. Here's what happened. In my first semester we had a marketing exam that concerned how to fill a sports centre during the daytime allowing for the fact that they tend to fill themselves during the evenings and weekends.

It just so happened that my dad had run countless sports centres during his early career and we owned one ourselves at one point. All of them did well. We had first hand experience of what works when you're trying to fill classes during the daytime. Your basic problem is that most people are at work during the day so it's best

"That's interesting, sir. I never realised marsupials were actually reptiles.
I'll remember to mention that in my next assignment."

to look somewhere other than the general workforce. If you target elderly, retired customers who are looking to keep fit that's half the battle. They have time on their hands and money to spend. Other things like advertising at jobcentres where there are a lot of unemployed people who have time during the day tend to work well also.

Perfectly logical and, from experience, a sound strategy that will bring results. Not in the textbook though. When the results came in my worst mark was marketing. Apparently that isn't how you fill a sports centre during the day. Even though it is, because it works. Do you see the conflict here?

Can't complain though. It reminded me that you've got to find out what they want and then give it to them. You've got to play the game. Stop trying to be original and start trying to find out what the person marking the papers thinks about the topics. It's far more effective. Of course I'm only human, and found it much easier to accept the lecturer's view when it didn't conflict with my own. To do it you need to give up a few things. If you're highly opinionated then that's going to be a problem. When push comes to shove you've got to become subordinate to the bosses' views. It's no use being confident and headstrong and wanting to change the world. Do it afterwards.

I kept my eyes on the prize and my opinions separate from the task in hand. There really isn't an easier way to convince someone you're good at something than fulfilling their exact perception of what is good. Try to find out what they think the right answer is and then agree with it. Valuable sentence, that one.

Much more useful than 'just work hard'. I had a friend who'd done really well in his course and had moved on to a great job on the back of it. I asked him how he did it, and his answer was "'bout all I did was stick with it". Marvellous and useless all at the same time.

Choosing modules

Another part of playing the game is to choose your modules tactically according to more than just what you find interesting and, strangely, what you think could be useful in future. I'd done both on the law course and it really hadn't worked out, largely due to the fact that the courses were never really as interesting as I'd hoped they'd be.

We decided to do it differently on the MBA. We took into account lots of different things. What we found interesting was ruthlessly placed at the bottom of the priority list.

- Firstly we looked at who would be marking the work. This is crucial because if you don't get on with the lecturers you'll find it difficult to build up enough of a relationship and rapport for them to be willing to give you their time and help. They know what the answer is and you have to try and get that out of them. This is always a more productive challenge if they are happy to talk to you.

- Then we looked at who else was taking the course. We tried to stick to taking the same modules because then the teamwork factor could give us an advantage. If all your potential team mates are taking different modules then strongly consider whether you can be successful on your own.

Then we needed to go one level above this. Look at the whole group. Is it a group you can see being successful together? Are there enough people in the class who will talk and argue points to the level that's necessary to be successful? We looked at all the groups and classes that were forming and tried to consider if the dynamic would be right. Basically, is the group going to sing or will it rival a family funeral for atmosphere every time you go into lectures? Also, more often than not we found that it's the people that make the class interesting, not the subject. Bear this in mind.

2

Understanding

If everything we did was designed to put us in the top bracket then it started with making sure we had a solid understanding of the work. So we considered how to ensure we had the best possible understanding of the theories we were being exposed to. Our process had its foundations in attendance. Nothing groundbreaking in that, is there? Needs to be said though.

We attended every lecture and seminar for the whole course save a few exceptional circumstances. Illness, incidentally, was never one of these. The basic principle of going to every lecture has the benefit that you tend to acquire the understanding as a matter of course. It doesn't take a lot of effort or intelligence to understand what's going on if you're always there. Attendance really is the best way to avoid failing, so if you're someone trying to avoid a third this is *the* key to doing that.

Admittedly we had a very strong personal motivation in that we

"Close your eyes. Relax. Listen to the voice.
$2x + 4y^2 = 8\pi$" where " is equivalent to..."

had simply paid too much money not to turn up. The issue of 'just not feeling like going' didn't come into play. Nevertheless full attendance played an enormous part in freeing time up to work productively on other things, rather than having to re-read things or cram because we didn't understand what was being discussed.

One important point to make is that nobody is going to understand everything, so don't be afraid to use the words 'I don't know' or admit you've never heard of a concept before. It's only the major stuff that you need to put up a front for. Try to use your judgement to see when you will get more benefit from asking about something rather than trying to bluff. We had one seminar that went on for two hours about how much companies should be spending on research and development and planning for the future. In the last five minutes of the class one lad stuck his arm in the air and came out with the immortal question, "What's R & D?". It rendered me useless for the remainder of the seminar.

It pays to be the best

Being among the best students in terms of understanding had a number of benefits. We could talk more in class which helped us learn. Discussion is the best form of learning for me. Understanding the subject removes the fear of looking stupid in public, which dramatically increases the likelihood that you'll ask questions and participate in lectures and seminars.

This is crucial because it's the first stage in projecting the impression that you're among the best students on the course. This is in your best interests if you're trying to get a First. We also did the lion's share of the presentations on the course. Again, this ensured that we had to be prepared otherwise people would have been able to see through us straight away. It was sort of enforced study.

We also made a big point of getting through as much of the reading lists as possible. This gives you the basics. To enhance this understanding we read current books that gave us a wider viewpoint. This is part of the slog that is needed but, as you'll see, there's a lot more to it than this. Having said that, it is utterly necessary to have a good level of understanding to allow you the chance of getting a First.

Openness

The next thing you need to realise is something that may well be beyond comprehension for many high achievers. You need to be willing to give all your work away. It's that simple. It's alright; you can come out from behind the sofa now. There's nothing to be afraid of. I believe that's one of the key reasons for my success, and possibly the overriding factor behind my finishing as number one: I was not one man's efforts. Nor was I the result of a collaboration between me and my brother. Nor still was I the result of collaboration between a close group of friends on the course.

In actuality I was the end result of small collaborations with just about *everyone* on the course. That's right, *everybody.* Throughout the course I was helped by the majority of people I was studying with. People gave me little titbits of information all the time and this built up to make me the most informed person on the course on just about everything we did.

This became perpetual, because as the course progressed people actually helped me more. Why on earth would anyone go out of their way to help the highest grade on the course? The answer is simple and you probably realise it yourself: most of the time I had actually helped them first.

The networking principle

What I'd later find out is one of the foundations of networking was the reason I was being helped by most people on the course. I'm a naturally helpful person, and I have grown out of wanting to be independent and succeed on my own. I did that on my law degree and look where it got me. I'm also a very open person. I don't believe in keeping good things to myself or in withholding information that I know is going to be helpful to others.

●

I was open with everything. You name it. I let colleagues read my work. I even gave them copies.

●

This is the reason that I was on the receiving end of such a waterfall of helpful insights from my colleagues on the course. From the outset I helped everyone I could in any way I could. It was irrelevant whether that included getting a reference for someone or talking people through what I was doing for the assignments and why. Even helping people move house and telling them where the best restaurants in the city were. It didn't matter. The fact that I helped them put me in everyone's good books. I did everything possible short of writing the essays for them.

I was open with everything. You name it. I let colleagues read my work. I even gave them copies. Often this was my own suggestion. I'd proof read essays; I'd do research for people; I presented work when other people didn't want to; I showed people where to look for research; I gave people passwords to my research accounts (I still do this); I suggested helpful articles; I handed over copies of my entire research for each and every module; I insisted that people include leading articles when they didn't realise that those articles were important; I counselled people; I held one-to-one panic meetings when some people didn't know what to do or didn't understand what had gone wrong. I even skipped class once to give a lift to a friend who thought the gas hob had been left on and the house could explode at any minute. I did all those things and more.

Why, you ask, go to such great lengths to help people? Like I said, I'm naturally helpful, but there is also an underhand motivation to my kindness that can't be ignored. I knew that these people would then help me when I asked them. I knew that they'd help me even when I didn't ask. I knew that my spontaneous help would result in spontaneous help in my direction at a later stage.

More blessed to give than to receive

My point is that I received little bits of help from everyone and this greatly increased my chances of getting a First. It didn't matter that in the majority of situations I was giving far more than I was receiving. The beauty was that the imbalance of help actually got more outweighed as the course went on. I was often doing work with nothing coming back my way. But that was only from a very narrow viewpoint. In the bigger picture, I was getting more help than anyone else on the course. But it wasn't help from one almighty source, it was much better than that. I was getting helped in little ways by everyone and it was making me and my product far stronger.

Exactly how I did this has much to do with the advances in technology that we have benefited from recently. I had invested in a superb PC that contained a CD-Rewriter. Wonderful things. They allowed me to transfer all the research and writing I'd done on all my modules onto discs that cost me 18p. I gave these discs to loads of people on the course. The look of slight surprise and delight that I received from the people I gave the discs to spurred me to do it as often as I could. It's an instant relationship builder in one easy step. Once you've got that relationship, you've not only acquired an ally and friend on the course but you've also gained another little tributary in your river of knowledge. I was still getting help on the last day before my dissertation deadline which signified the end of the course.

In the second semester, as my openness began to infect my colleagues, they started taking me to one side and showing me avenues of research that were absolute goldmines. Journals I never knew existed, books I'd never even heard of. I was getting help from everyone. You must seek to build such a network on your course. It is a massive help and one of the key reasons behind my success.

"Tell you what: you hand over your research, your essays and all your reference books. And I'll lend you my pencil."

For some this won't be easy, and will feel unnatural. It is important that you accept that openness is the *easiest* policy for getting a First. Lock ego and selfishness away for the duration of your course and you make it far easier for yourself to achieve your goal. Another realisation is that you must never be afraid to ask for help. Pride must go in the same locker if it's going to stop you seeking help from colleagues.

Yet another realisation is that I really did ask for help from everyone. This included people who failed the module. Everyone has something to give you even if it's the most insignificant thing. I never looked upon people in terms of how they performed in assessment because in life I think assessments do not give a true reflection of people's talents or capacities. I wanted to learn from everyone regardless of their apparent level of knowledge on the subject and I knew they all held some benefit that would bring me a greater chance of success. It was so far and away the best decision I ever made, it's frightening.

A word of warning

One issue to be aware of is that this open policy potentially poses the problem of people plagiarising your work and landing you both in trouble. This happened on my course but, quite remarkably, not to me. A Greek friend, Antonios, had written an excellent IT strategy essay for one of the modules we'd done and had received a mark of 80 for his troubles.

The problem was that one of our Nigerian friends, who shall remain anonymous (this isn't name and shame), had been stuck as to what to do for this particular assignment and had pleaded to see Antonios' essay to give him an idea of what to do. Antonios had agreed and very kindly allowed our Nigerian friend a copy of this remarkable essay. Unfortunately our friend made the mistake of cutting and pasting two graphs directly out of Antonios' work which was promptly spotted by the marker, and both would have received zero had the rules been strictly adhered to. In the event Antonios eventually had his mark restored to the full 80 and our friend bore the brunt of the punishment for the mistake.

This is a lesson that should be learnt well. You must judge whether the people you give your work to are likely to heed the warnings that they must not copy the work. That really comes down to trust. I made this point expressly every time I gave the work, and after the above case took to physically writing it on the disk front as proof; dated and signed.

4

Time Management

The course I took (an MBA) is one of the hardest courses, if not the hardest, that any university offers in terms of the amount of work that you're expected to do. They throw deadlines and examinations at you for the entire duration of the course. There's hardly time to breathe because it gets so hectic. I made every deadline for every assignment I was given on the course. I saw this as a matter of discipline and was of the opinion that if I was trying to project the image that I was among the best on the course then things like extensions due to extenuating circumstances would not help my cause.

Other people on the course did not make all the deadlines. Some missed deadlines regularly and always seemed to have a fully understandable excuse. In the long run this approach will not get you where you want to be. Whether you get a First or not inevitably comes down to a decision by your course tutors and supervisors, and as I say throughout this book, it's important you

"Sleeping, shopping, socialising, computer games, drinking... Hmmm.
That leaves from 4pm until 4.10 for work."

don't load them with ammunition that will allow them to come up with too many reasons why you don't merit a first class mark.

I found that when it comes to time management it is a waste of time planning things to the minutest detail because plans always change no matter how hard you try. That's life, as they say. Frank Sinatra probably said it best, but that's another matter. You'll overrun on some things which will mean that everything else has to be restructured to accommodate this, so you find that you constantly have to devote time to planning rather than to working.

Stay loose

I found that a loose structure is the best approach to planning your work. I tried to assess how much work I had to do and by what deadlines. Then it's a case of prioritising. I tried to stick to the old adage 'first things first' when I planned my work. By that I mean invariably I did the work for the immediate next deadline.

This may sound common sense to you but even on a course as demanding as the MBA I was amazed to see people devoting enormous amounts of time to work that didn't need to be in for months. This was often done to the neglect of the pressing task. I strongly advise against this approach. My background is in the world of professional sport and I find it hard to stray from the view that the most important game is the next one. Try to juggle deadlines and have one eye on work that isn't due in for a while and you find that you lose focus on your immediate task.

When you're considering your time management take this next point into consideration. There is such a thing as 'the zone' when it comes to writing assignments. I found that when I structured my work in blocks, and directed all my attention to the work that was due in next, I was able to get into that zone far more easily than if I tried to balance two or three assignments and make progress on all of them. The main benefit I received from this was that I was into the flow of each essay and knew where to look for documents I'd downloaded and how each document was going to help me build a well supported argument.

The time that this saves is why I followed the block approach. Without it you are constantly searching for references and sentences you know you need but you can't remember where they are or which file they're in. That pushes up the time you need to do each essay and when you consider that you may have a lot of essays then managing your time well is crucial to getting a First.

One of the main reasons I didn't do well at my law degree was that I'd find myself running out of time. A key to avoiding a Third, or a Fail, is making sure that you've got the time you'll need to produce a decent piece of work. Successfully having enough time for each piece of work is half the battle, but add on top of that the ability to really maximise how you're using that time and you're almost there.

Work smarter, not harder

The secret is that I didn't spend more time than anybody else when it came to doing work. I know lots of the other students had to spend far more time than I did on the exact same pieces of work and during my law degree I'd subscribed to the philosophy that the good students must be doing more work than me. But that's not the answer.

The key is being highly productive when you do work. I found the block approach to be the most productive and effective way of writing assignments. This is one of the key reasons why I decided to write this book. I wanted to dispel the myth that it's the students that do the most work who get the best marks. It's a total fabrication. The students that find the best balance between productivity and time will stand a far better chance of doing well than those who just try to do more work.

I also found that in a certain way, the less work I did the more productive I became. I was doing less work but I was sharper when I did it and took more in whilst churning more out. I tried to do little bits at a time and stop my head from overloading. Little short bursts instead of the traditional long slogs.

I wanted to dispel the myth that it's the students that do the most work who get the best marks.

Manchester United use the same approach. They train at high intensity for short periods. Everyone is conditioned to be sharper when they work and they play better because of it. Your academic study is not dissimilar. Keep your head fresh by doing short bursts rather than long slogs and you will be able to get more done and at a higher quality. Leave the sleep deprivation tests to people in the army.

This is something I've learnt through experience. For my undergraduate degree I used to spend hours and hours in the library trying to work. Trouble was, I find it difficult to stay awake in the library. This is no joke. Alright, I'll confess. My trick was to position myself just at the end of the little cubicle with a book directly in front of me. Then I'd lean my head against the side and no one could see that I was sleeping instead of reading the book. After a month I found I couldn't stop this addiction to sleeping on the job.

To counter my remarkable sleeping habits, I found on the MBA course that if I limited my time to little hour long slots in different places then I was actually doing the work. I'd read in the library, car, bedroom, car park, riverside, café, bar, anywhere that was new. The fact that I was keeping the environment fresh meant that I wasn't getting sick of the same old view every time I wanted to work. This helped enormously to keep my enthusiasm for the Distinction alive.

I also planned my time with a built in break from each piece of work. I found that when I left the work and did something entirely different for a while I was sharper when I went back to it to finish it off. I found it easy to spot the mistakes in my writing and, more importantly, I found it easier to spot the gaps in my argument.

I often found that when I went back to my work I would change the structure to give the work a more logical flow. This process of thinking what the logical structure to the essay was helped to highlight the missing parts of the argument that really should be included. Due to the particular course I took, the MBA, it became inevitable that as soon as I left one piece of work I had to start on another for some other module because of time constraints. Nevertheless the break from that specific piece of work always helped.

5

Investment

You must be prepared to invest financially to get a First. My brother and I cut no corners and were in by far the best postion to get a First of anyone on the course. It's like Manchester United. Their Carrington training ground is on another level from the training facilities that the other clubs have. They have all the facilities that you could ever wish for, and this puts them in the best position possible to be number one in the league, and in the world for that matter.

It's not that having better jacuzzis or indoor pitches or training kit or sleeping areas could each account for their success on its own. You'd be pushed to single out one thing. But the whole package they've put in place *does* make a difference. It changes everything.

We've often said that if players are given the best facilities it makes them feel world class. It changes their mindset when they turn up each day. They have the confidence of knowing that they have advantages over the competition. This is a sporting example but life is no different in any other profession. We treated our education the same way. It's not cheap though. We had an unlimited expense account and had already exceeded that by the fourth month.

PC power

We both bought fast PCs and had the full Microsoft Office suite on both. The computers were less expensive because we had them made rather than going to somewhere like PC World and paying off-the-shelf prices. We also invested in broadband internet access. This let us download lecture notes from the university website in seconds.

Once we had the notes, we had the software to let us sit and take mini lectures in double quick time by going through the lecture slides on Microsoft PowerPoint. We could make our presentations look professional with PowerPoint and this helped give everyone on the course, particularly the lecturers, the impression that we were switched on. We each had an all in one printer/scanner which let us print off the lecture notes as and when we wanted, and we could copy other people's notes overnight and give them back the next day.

Most importantly we had the ability to do research on databases from home at the click of a button. While the other students were having to sit in the university computer rooms and wait an eternity to download articles and course notes, we could keep fresh and do more work in 20 minutes than they could do in an entire evening.

Our effectiveness went through the roof. One improvement that you could make would be to get a laptop and have more flexibility than we did. The time we saved in downloading through broadband rather than through an ordinary modem connection meant that we were able to do more work than anybody else in a fraction of the time, giving us more time off to do other things.

Get the benefit of books

We then set about trying to buy the books recommended in the reading lists. Having your own copies is a must because the library is invariably out of stock when you need books the most. One of the main points that came across from our time on the course is that you need to be able to show you conducted wider reading than just the books set out on the reading lists.

To serve this demand we made a point of haunting local book stores to see if there was anything that would be of any use. Once you've freed up funds to do it, you'll generally find that bookstores are goldmines for the wider reading you need to show to get a First. Be prepared to invest.

In the first month I became a member of amazon.co.uk. It really is the best internet website there is. At the start of each module I'd quickly log on to Amazon and type in words that I'd used to search the databases the university provides you with. The results never ceased to amaze me, particularly for my dissertation which was on teamwork. I am now the proud owner of possibly the world's foremost private library on books regarding teamwork and teamworking and it's all due to Amazon. I'd never have found the rich collection of books I needed without Amazon, and I recommend that you pursue a similar path.

Check your sources

We also subscribed to independent sources of information. ft.com and economist.com are both examples of this. Both have articles covering a wide range of topics and both will help give your study credibility because they are respected sources. They have an obvious benefit for business students but their database has enough to cover a huge number of topics. I was living with a couple of student mates, one of whom was studying for a law degree. We searched ft.com out of curiosity and he went into his next exam with stacks of independent analysis that was up to date and relevant.

In your particular course you need to find similar sources for references and independent information because it's all part of showing the wider reading that is so important in differentiating yourself from everybody else. The wider reading thing is a big hang-up for universities, and can make a convincing argument for getting a 2:2 rather than a third. Making an investment here can have a huge effect on pulling your marks up if you're at the lower end of the scale.

"I just wish I could find the 'on' switch."

Get out and about

Another thing that made us better prepared than most was that we attended seminars around the country on the topics that we were studying. In our second semester we found out that Tom Peters, one of the world's foremost business thinkers, was holding a conference on leadership in Manchester. That would be great, we thought, for showing wider reading and for showing we were up to date. We would be getting it from the horse's mouth so to speak. He was on stage for most of the day (nine to five, which was impressive) and we got great material for many of our assignments.

Even better than that, we noticed that at the intervals Tom Peters was standing at the side of the stage alone and seemingly looking for something to do. Confidence has never been a problem for us, so while the 650 or so other visitors were getting tea, we had a personal conversation about our essays with one of the authors of *In Search of Excellence*. Fabulous! It doesn't come much better than that really.

We also managed to get invited, by a friend on our course, to a seminar at Oxford University that was called *Success: Art or Science?* It's an event that is organised by the Oxford MBA students to get leading people from around the world to come and talk to them about business. It was one of the best seminars I've ever been to and was a fantastic experience. We again came away with material that would turn out to be useful for most of the essays we would write from then until the end of the course.

The important point is that we had made sure we were in as good a situation as anyone on the course. We couldn't really be bettered in terms of effectiveness. We manufactured a position where we had the best resources and the best capacity to find resources. This played a large part in keeping Stephen and me ahead of the game.

6

Talent

There is no escaping it. In order to get a First you need to be capable of balancing arguments effectively. For some people this is not possible and their talents lie in other areas. That is not to say that in using this strategy they couldn't benefit, because this approach will improve your mark regardless of your ability.

I only want to state the obvious that you need to have *some* talent for academia before you start trying to aim too high. You don't need to be the *most* talented (I'm living proof) but in order to aim for a First or a Distinction you need to realise that it is a combination of inspiration and perspiration. Without a little of the inspiration you are not setting a realistic goal to aim to be top or among the top group.

But it's certainly not everything. I did alright at law considering everyone else on the course had got into the uni with AAA at A-levels. I had got BCCE for mine, and the only reason I was on the

"I'm doing my dissertation on Renaissance attitudes to humility.
It's a subject I have a natural gift for."

course was that I was a transfer. A change of circumstance had meant I couldn't stay at my first university and had to transfer to a local one when I moved. Happily for me, it was a much better law course on paper according to the rankings, but I found them about the same in practice.

My point is that I was on a course with people who were supposedly far more academically talented, and supposedly more intelligent, than myself. The university had gone to great lengths to make sure that the entry standards were very high specifically to keep people like me out of their courses.

Yet I was not struggling on the course by any means. Far from it. Granted, I wasn't the best there, but I didn't embarrass myself. Ultimately what I'm arguing here is that despite the imbalance in talent that my case presented, the results didn't show that imbalance. I was mid-table, which meant I had to be getting better marks than half the people who actually got AAA at A-level. It shows that talent is just one of the factors to affect how well you can do, and if you counterbalance ordinary talent with quality in some other department, you can still come out with a First in the end.

7

Lifestyle

Another thing you can't escape. A normal person can't get a good degree *and* be drunk every night of the week for the whole course. It may be possible, but I'd suggest that those who can achieve it have outright natural talent. With the amount of money riding on my passing you'll understand if I felt inclined not to try and disprove this theory (especially as I was clearly lacking in natural talent). Having said that, by no means did I give up my social life to any great extent. I led just as active a social life as a normal person who works a 9-5 job would. I was out drinking generally twice a week and filled many other evenings with normal social activities.

I imposed only a few restrictions on my normally free lifestyle. By my own admission, my ability to be sharp and bubbly and interact with other humans drops dramatically when I've been out drinking heavily the night before. So far I've yet to uncover the

"Right. According to my schedule I should be out enjoying myself in three and a half minutes."

reason behind this strange phenomenon, so answers on a post-card if you please.

When you're trying to create the perception that you're on the ball and know what you're talking about, you can't really drink the night before. This might just be me, but if I can get to the bathroom the next morning without crawling I'm doing well. This limited my drinking to Friday and Saturday nights.

Remarkably there is an entire country just off the coast of continental Europe known as the UK where you find nearly 60m people who also tend to want to enjoy themselves on a Friday and Saturday night. So nothing was really compromised there.

The only other real restriction was that I knuckled down a few weeks before exams and coursework deadlines and didn't go out much during these periods. I also didn't drink during these periods for safe measure. Those two little commitments are the only two things that affected my social life. If I'm honest they weren't big things and didn't make that much difference to my enjoying myself. If you want to be out more often than twice a week then money will tend to be more of a hindrance than your uni work so again it's not that big a restriction.

Importantly, when I went out I enjoyed myself. I hung on to the fact that I was doing all these different things to keep me ahead of the game, which stopped me feeling guilty when I was out. Should I be back at home doing work? Yes if I was doing uni in the same way as everybody else. But I wasn't doing it the same way, so I had a freedom that most don't enjoy.

8

Teamwork

Teamwork helped both me and my brother get Distinctions. It's that simple. To do it alone is a very difficult task and you need to have a lot of talent and commitment. Why not make it easier? If you split the workload and help each other out then you can free up time to enjoy yourself and relax.

We used the fact that we were twins to our advantage. As a first example, we split the reading list. Each week we'd read half of what we'd been told to read in full. As we had six modules per semester, this usually entailed me doing the reading for three of the modules in full while Stephen did the reading for the other three, and then we'd alternate modules every week.

But surely you're missing half the reading each week? Not so. Because we owned the books, we read each book armed with a highlighter and pen and we would highlight the important points while at the same time making little comments where a good thought had popped up. Then we could speed read the highlighted books from the other three modules each week and get the gist of what was being said.

●

Sharing the workload makes sense.

●

This saved an enormous amount of time and was one of the ways in which we fully justified investing the money in our own copies of the books. We got all the understanding with about 60% of the effort compared with other students who were spending relentless hours trying to keep up. Frankly, to do our reading list alone would be impossible in my opinion. It was massive. I fully recommend that you get a partner on your course for this specific reason. Sharing the workload makes sense.

Share the research

We also split the research tasks. There was no point in us both going out and spending time trying to find the same articles. We alternated that as well. Each week I'd do the research for three modules while Stephen did the other three. This again had the effect that we were actually doing less work than the others and looking far better prepared than anybody else.

Add to this the fact that we'd bought broadband and our research was more productive in any case, and you start to see how the benefits snowball. Also consider that because we had strong relationships with the other students we were getting their research as well, and you start to see how the plan fits together to put us in

"So that means I'll read 'Asterix the Gaul' and you read
Gibbon's 'Decline and Fall'."

a much better position than trying to do it as a one man mission, John Rambo style.

One of the key ways we split the research was on the actual assignments themselves. As well as knowing intricately what topic the other was doing, and so being able to look out for articles that would be useful, we gave each other the reference lists on assignments where we'd both been given the same task. This made our preparation for writing the essays much more effective.

Read each other's work

And once we'd written the assignments, we read each other's work and were able to give an informed but independent opinion about how to improve each other's essay. Several times we would catch gaps in essays; things that were missing which needed to be in but had been overlooked.

On one occasion we'd been given a task that was open to interpretation, but we needed to address three key models. For whatever reason, the third model had been overlooked on one of Stephen's essays. Everyone makes mistakes so you need to have procedures in place to catch them. Quality assurance, really.

In this particular case I only spotted it while we were printing out my essay to hand it in. Stephen quickly made the changes to include the comment needed on the third model and ended up receiving 81% for that particular essay. Without having caught the oversight, he wouldn't have been able to get a First because he'd have missed out a crucial part. Teamwork makes a difference.

The more people you can get involved in this process the better. For our dissertations there were three of us reading each other's essays. Two independent brains are better than one. In the preparation for our first exam there were six of us sitting round a table going through everyone's preparation to be sure that no one had overlooked the obvious. This was a great situation.

Getting a good mark has a lot to do with making sure that you haven't missed the obvious in any aspect. Don't make fundamental errors and you can't go far wrong. These meetings helped us eliminate those fundamental errors so that at least we all had a chance. It doesn't standardise everyone, it just ensures that everyone's still in the game. That included me so I ran with it.

To state the point again: teamwork helped us both get Distinctions. Too often the students who are trying to get Firsts are very secretive people. They play the game close to their chests and don't give much away. That's one way to do it but it wasn't our way. Our way is *much much* easier. It really is a situation where the end result will be more than the sum of the parts. I haven't made many express recommendations to you but I strongly suggest that you take this point on board. John Rambos don't come along very often. The rest of us do it together.

Ask what is expected

For each of our modules we were given an assessment that had a specific task. This is standard for nearly every course around the world, be it an MBA, Law, Science, Art, Geography, whatever. Your performance on the course will be judged primarily on your performance in that assessment, be it exam or assignment.

The way we went about these assessments was to have a strategy in place to try and maximise the chances of getting a Distinction. We went about this in a very specific way. Here it is. The assessments are set by the module tutors in most courses. So they are the people who are going to know what the answers are. We set out to talk with the module leaders on as regular a basis as we could.

We started this process by talking about the assessments in class and making a point of seizing opportunities at the end of lectures and seminars to grill the tutors about the assessment. What is it?

What's it going to be on? What's the format? How should we prepare? We asked all sorts of different questions that would give us a better insight into how to answer the questions that we would be asked. Then we spent five minutes writing it all down.

By the way, have a separate section in each file that is entirely dedicated to collecting knowledge on the assessment. This is the only way I made sure that we weren't losing crucial bits of information and that nothing would be overlooked. Come alive in lectures when you hear little sentences about the assessment, and keep noting it down it in your assessment section. When it comes to writing the answer you'll know where to start.

The talking process then progressed to talking to the other students. Like I mentioned in the section about openness, *everyone* has thoughts on how to best answer the question. Everyone has sources they are using, articles they've found, and so on, and it is priceless if you can gain access to such information.

Think about it. If I suggested a transfer of information, so they were to get all my research and I was to get all theirs, we would both be in a stronger position. In most cases they knew they would benefit from such an arrangement far more than me, so people were generally up for it. But I was moving forward and was in an even stronger position to do the same again with the next student and repeat the process and make another few little steps. A cunning plan based on helping others, wouldn't you agree?

"So, just between ourselves, could you tell me the
questions and the answers?"

Covert inquiries

Now here's the beauty of the plan. A bit of undercover private investigation. We met each module tutor in person on a one-to-one basis to ask specifically about the assessment. We met them twice where possible. The meetings served several purposes.

●

We tried to associate our work with Distinctions at every opportunity

●

Firstly they were the perfect opportunity to outline that we were trying to get Distinctions. This let them know about it, and as they were marking the work it made sense to be clear what we were trying to get out of the module. When they see your name on your coursework you have put the perception into the marker's mind that you're among the top students, and your work is among the best they'll see that year. It's sort of a halo effect.

We tried to associate our work with Distinctions at every opportunity so they would pick it up to mark it thinking, "I'll read one of the good ones first". They were reading our work with the preconception that it was first class standard, and would expect to justify this preconception. This, we thought, would be the best way to ensure passing the course (remember the origins of the plan).

Secondly the meetings seemed to be the clearest way to find out what the hell we were supposed to put in the answer. We asked questions like these:

- What are you expecting to see in the answer?
- What leading authorities are you expecting to see?
- Do you think there should be more article based references or more book based references?
- What balance do you like to see?
- What is the best structure for this answer?
- What would a good answer have in it?
- What will be missing in a bad answer?
- What will be the difference between a good answer and a Distinction?
- What are the main criteria for a Distinction?
- How will you mark the work?

We covered issues of presentation, structure, format; the whole works. One of the most important questions we asked was to do with the word limit. Is the tutor bothered about the word limit? This is one of the most important questions that we asked, because on more than one of our essays we found out that the tutor didn't care about the word limit as long as you didn't hand in work that rivalled the Old Testament in length.

We took advantage of this fact to pack more into our essays than those who tried to stick to the set word limit. I made a point of keeping emails that I'd received that said they weren't bothered about word limit though, because you never know when things may go wrong and you need to be able to have more than, "Well, she said it was alright". Cover yourself. It's *Godfather* tactics – you don't want to come out of the toilets firing with just your dick in your hands.

Lessons from history

Thirdly we got the chance to ask whether or not we could see previous answers that had got Distinctions. This was invaluable when we did get to see them because it made expressly clear what standard would be expected. When you're looking through them make sure you're trying to spot how you can better them.

On one module I read four Distinction essays that were bloody excellent and would prove hard to top. But there were areas I felt we could beat them in. I thought we could beat them on presentation, depth of information and variety of sources. Interestingly they all had a very similar format to their answers and the question we had been set was similar to theirs. So we made our changes but kept largely to their format because we knew it was on the money.

I also used the opportunity to look through their reference lists and see what sources they had used. Some of the best and most fruitful avenues of research were started through ideas I got from those first class essays.

True to form I also had a look at essays that got bad marks. They were invariably haphazard. Things didn't fit with one another, they had no real structure and approached the question in a shotgun manner, just trying to put as much information down as possible in the hope that some of it might be relevant.

A good tip for avoiding a bad mark is to make sure that you've paid attention to more than just the information you're presenting. Also look at how you're presenting it and in what order.

You'd be surprised how a bad essay can be turned round by simply introducing a logical progression to the argument.

Simply the best

As a point of note, make sure you get to see dissertations that got Firsts. I saw five. I made full copies of each of them even though it took me a day to do. Most libraries will stock past dissertations and most courses will suggest you go and read ones on similar topics to yours.

I had problems with this suggestion. I wanted to read the dissertations that had received the best marks. I learnt far more about writing a good dissertation from the five dissertations I copied, which had absolutely nothing to do with my chosen topic, than I did from any of the dissertations on similar topics.

I asked all the lecturers I could whether they remembered, or were prepared to show me, which dissertations had received the best marks. As it transpired only one lecturer (who would eventually become my supervisor) was kind enough to give me this crucial information and I was subsequently delighted to be able to hand him a Distinction standard dissertation because of it. An inspired trade. He gives me the information and I deliver a dissertation that is Distinction standard for him to mark. This makes him look a great supervisor, which he was, and everyone has benefited.

So there's a key part of our plan in plain English. Hunt down the people who are marking your work, ask them what they are looking for, and then give it to them. My father, a sports conditioning coach, used to say about training his athletes *"Find out what makes them tick. Find out what they want, then prescribe it to them"*. Never was this advice more applicable than on our course.

Referencing

Your university will have its own favoured style of referencing (be it Legal, Harvard or otherwise). Invest time in finding out the correct way of doing whichever style you're required to do. Doing it well may not bring you extra marks, but doing it badly will almost certainly cost you marks.

This happened to me on one of my assignments and was undoubtedly a factor in the final mark. It's a matter of not giving your marker the ammunition to build a case against giving you a First. The less ammunition you offer, the less chance that you'll be marked down. Referencing definitely falls into this ammunition category so make sure you're on the ball.

Now I would like to introduce you to a little secret of mine. I call it the 'purple page' method. First it is important to make a rather obvious observation. In a general context, heavily referenced essays stand a better chance of getting a First than essays with a

"Yes the references are extensive, I grant you. But that's all you've given me. Where's the rest of the essay?"

standard level of referencing. Similar to the point made about referencing style, good referencing alone won't get you a First, but poorly referenced work will stop you getting one. Excellent referencing in a piece of work is ammunition for your marker to award a First. So you can regard it as a contributing factor.

Having said that, what often happens is that your lecturers will tell you how to set out your references, and then fail to explain what type of references to use: amount? Source? Contemporary?

The purple page

Here's what I know about referencing. Now I get to explain the purple page method. It's such a great cheat. The purple page method concerns the level of referencing that is contained in your assignment. I always worked on the premise that the more referencing I had in any given essay, the more chance to convince the marker that this essay was referenced well enough to merit a first class mark. Because that's what's important here. Let's make that aim nice and clear. This implies that the level of referencing in your work needs to be better than that of all the other people on your course. OK, maybe all is going too far, but it absolutely must be among the best group of assignments on your course.

●

Good referencing alone won't get you a First, but poorly referenced work will stop you getting one

●

The purple page method involves using Microsoft Word's

wonderful highlighter feature. It entails highlighting all the references in your assignment in purple. Then use the zoom feature to view the entire page and document. Basically, if every paragraph has a wealth of purple highlighted references, then we're on track. An example is this:

> Tesco have made the growth of their international operations a fundamental part of their overall business strategy (Annual Review, 2001). Sir Terry Leahy, Tesco's CEO, introduced the strategy of overseas expansion in emerging markets (Annual Report, 2001) and Tesco are now reaping the benefits of these ventures (Voyle, 2002). Tesco has the fastest organic growth of any major international retailer (Mintel, 2002). Independent analysts hold Tesco's international success in high regard (Lex Column, 2002), and new market entry is again on the horizon (Lex Column, 2002, Mintel, 2002).

This is the sort of level that you need to be looking at for every referenced paragraph. The beauty of the method is that it becomes wonderfully easy to spot where you've made a point without citing any authority. Sometimes I'd zoom out at quite a late stage in the writing of an essay (with the deadline starting to loom over me) and find that I'd written a decent paragraph that made a great point but had absolutely nothing to back it up. Flowery waffle.

The purple page technique gave me the ability, otherwise difficult to achieve, to correct these mistakes and, believe me, once you've started to use 'purple page' you'll understand how easily it lets you uncover and correct these 'floating in limbo' paragraphs.

Think of them as parasites, hiding amongst otherwise productive sections.

Quality as well as quantity

The next important point concerning referencing is that you must pay attention to who it is you're referencing. Spend time trying to unearth the leading authorities in the area your assignment's on. You must include the leading authorities because the marker will be aware of who they are and will be expecting to see that you've considered their views. And believe me; finding out who they are is rarely rocket science. The leading authorities usually stand out like a sore thumb once you've set out to find them. To be sure, we asked the lecturers to point us in the right direction and found that they were generally very helpful.

As well as being relevant, it's important that the references show a balance between being up-to-date and historically significant. What I mean here is that you need to show that you are aware of the current thinking on the subject, but also aware of the landmark authorities that have been around for years. This will be the same for just about every course offered at colleges and universities all over the world.

The being contemporary thing I addressed by limiting my searches on the internet databases to the current year. I did the same for amazon.co.uk and enjoyed great success with both. It's always good to be able to pepper your work with references from the current year because it shows you're up to date and it may be giving the marker knowledge they'd previously been unaware of, which helps impress on them that your work is worthy of a First. Our independent sources, such as ft.com, helped lend these newer references credibility.

The historically significant references are the ones that we found cropped up in most other students' reference lists and were those mentioned as elementary by lecturers in class. We referenced these but never heavily. It's about showing you know of them, and have considered the argument they make, but you then move on quickly to the discussion of how the newer ones relate to the old ones.

Safety in numbers

The sheer number of references that we compiled was something we paid close attention to. I saw it as a way to differentiate ourselves from the other students and also to show that we'd put in the amount of work necessary to get a First. We had more references in our assignments than any other that I saw. That includes other students' work on our course, and answers from years gone by.

For one module assignment the lecturer had suggested that having 10-12 good references would be sufficient. We submitted papers that contained in excess of 100 separate sources. I saw work from other students who were getting good marks and found that they'd had the same sort of idea and had references lists with 50+ sources. I still believe that it was to our advantage to show the marker that we had gone to far greater lengths than anybody else. It's the only way to get a positive reaction from a reference list. The last thing you want when they consider your references is that they think 'standard'. Everything about your work should say that this is the best of the group and the number of quality references is no exception.

It's worth noting that we simply wouldn't have been able to do this for every essay if we hadn't been getting the benefits of both broadband internet access and other people feeding us good sources from their research. We consistently handed in essays with over 100 separate sources and both found over 160 sources for our dissertations. That's well in excess of 1,200 references over the duration of the course and to do that you need to have broadband and a strong network in place. I don't see any other realistic way to get to the same level.

Breadth as well as depth

Another important point to note is that we tried to avoid the possibility that the marker would pull us up for relying too heavily on a small number of sources. To make sure that this didn't happen we made a point of never having a reference the same as the one that preceded it. It helps keep the references fresh and stops you running the same sources into the ground.

Again, this probably didn't positively affect the marking but it certainly avoided another possible negative that the marker could use as ammunition for not giving us a First. It's like trying to make sure that your team doesn't rely too heavily on one or two players for goals. If you've got lots of players who can get involved then the team has a more solid foundation. Essays are the same.

There's another confession here. I didn't actually read every book I referenced. Not even every article. It's impossible. Anyone who's tried to do it will tell you the same. Secretly I suspect that every lecturer in the world knows it as well. They're just not telling. It isn't humanly possible to read every page of every reference you use and still be as well referenced as you should be. It's a question of skimming through, getting the gist of their argument and picking out a couple of choice sentences which you can use to support your argument.

Trying to do any more than that is giving yourself a challenge with no reward if you succeed. In fact, although it sounds crazy, it would be a serious disadvantage to try and complete all the reading you need to do. You'd use up time that would be better spent working on your argument and structure. I'm glad I've got that off my chest.

The only time I varied this method was when I knew that the lecturer had written the book I was referencing or discussing. In that instance, you'd better make sure that you know what you're talking about. The chance of them seeing through a skim over reference is far greater so I tried to stay on my guard and spend a bit of time going over the whole of the book. It just seemed to make sense.

Assignment schedule

We used the same process for each piece of work we were given. We put a lot of thought into what would be the best way to go about an assignment and once we had a structure we were happy with we used it for every assignment.

Our basic approach was as follows:

1 Questions about the assignment in lectures

These were usually at the end of class. "Tell us more about the assignment" was used at every lecture as a matter of course. When we caught them in a good mood they told us more. Funny that, isn't it?

2 Choose topic

Some assignments offered a number of alternatives. When this was the case we tried to make the decision as early as possible so we could spend the rest of the semester collecting little sentences that were relevant from each of the lectures.

3 Begin literature collection

We started with the elementary searches, getting the texts on the reading lists etc. We'd then go through the library catalogue and see what came up. The university databases have loads of articles so this was our next port of call. There was usually enough there to keep us busy for the whole semester.

4 Questions among the other students for their approaches

"How are the other students approaching it?". We tried to get a general opinion of the best view. This is very much an 'ask the audience' source of information. If lots of people are doing it one way, more often than not it's a good way to start.

5 Questions in class about our topic

We then started to ask more focused questions about our specific topics. Don't be afraid to do this in class because other students who are doing the same topic will often join in. When this happened we got the group pressure thing going on.

6 Begin reading

This can't be avoided. Our understanding was greatly improved by reading the books and articles. If anyone has found a way round this, let me know. We did try to limit the reading as much as we could. I read three large books cover to cover, beyond that I tried to pick and choose wisely the chapters I read. It's a question of biting the bullet when you know there isn't a short cut.

7 Draft structure to assignment

Early on we tried to set a structure so that we knew what we were aiming at. Once we'd done this we could collect information that was tailored to our needs rather than generalised.

8 Meet with tutor and discuss how to get a Distinction

Once we'd set a basic structure and we'd done a fair bit of reading, we felt we were in a position to go and see the tutors and ask the right questions. We could show our understanding quickly and move the conversation on to discussing the finer points that would make a difference and give us an insight. Invaluable.

9 Collect other students' tips and resources

As I mentioned earlier, if everyone is doing it one way then this is a good indication that it's close to the target. We'd talk to as many people as we could and get their suggestions. We discovered lots of research avenues from these conversations.

10 Begin writing

We felt that at this stage, having done the groundwork and having met the tutor and heard what they'd like, we could realistically start writing and know that we'd not have to scrap it because it was shite. Basically we knew we wouldn't be wasting our time putting effort into something that would turn out to be useless.

11 Exhaust literature research

Only once we'd started writing did we start to get a feel for what was missing and what the heart of the essay would be. Once

*you've got that then go back to your sources and find more refer-
ences to really add depth to the work. We could be even more specific in our searches by this stage.*

12 Finish all reading

*There does come a time when it's best to cut loose and move on.
Only you can judge when this stage is but make sure that you're
confident that you have sufficient understanding to produce first
class work.*

13 Draft final essay

*At this stage we had everything in place to let us write a
Distinction level essay. It was a question of putting all the pieces
together. We'd done the homework to find out what was expected,
we'd done the research, we'd been given loads of help from the
other students and now we could be confident that we'd covered all
bases in terms of preparation. The chances of a first class result
are more to do with the preparation than the actual writing.*

14 Independent reading by third party

*Once we'd written a draft that incorporated all the aspects of our
preparation we needed to have a third party proof read the work
and then make comments. In our case, because we tried to do similar assignments and maximise the amount of help we could give
each other, we were in an informed position to give comment. We
knew the topic inside out so we could suggest additions that would
not be possible if the third party is reading the assignment blind
(i.e. without knowing the topic well).*

"I can't see where our two week gambling research trip to
Vegas fits into this schedule..."

15   Revisit structure (What's missing? Is this the best way? Etc)

Once we'd looked at improvements in the argument, we turned our attention to looking at the structure to see if it was still the best way to present the work. Often there were changes that gave the assignments more of a flow. This is about trying to maintain the consistency of argument that is needed in a first class piece of work. Everything needs to have a logical progression. The best way we found was to do this both at the start and at the end of the process because things can change.

16   Make final adjustments

We really just set this time aside to tidy up the loose ends. References that were missing, sentences we weren't happy with etc. This takes longer than you'd think so we tried to set aside at least a day.

17   Reference drive

Once we'd written the whole piece, and once we'd made the changes so that it was essentially capable of being handed in, we set out to give it as much support as we could. We'd check the references, make sure that we hadn't relied on a select few too often, and then we'd set about trying to fit as many in as we could. In accordance with the purple page strategy, we'd try to make the document as heavily referenced as possible. I've never heard anyone fail because they had too much support. The more the merrier.

18   Finish reference list and bibliography

This took forever. I can honestly name 1,001 things I'd rather do but it does make a difference and you need to do it properly. We'd go through and check that all the references in the references list were actually in the document itself; all other supporting articles we hadn't used as references went in the bibliography.

19 Print in colour on good paper

We found a good quality printer and then paid a bit extra to have it in colour and on good quality paper. It just fits with the rest of the strategy.

20 Get assignment bound

Same as the paper, this was very much a 'get your hand in your pocket' situation. Pay more and it'll look better. Again, it just fits with everything else.

21 Hand in

At this point I liked to go out and celebrate like it was 1999. Have a good night. When the whistle's been blown it's out of your hands.

This just about covers the way we went about each essay. The approach was designed to make sure that all our bases were covered. We felt that working to this structure would be putting our efforts into a logical process that had a good chance of getting us a First. It takes account of the groundwork necessary to ensure that you're spending time on productive work, and also builds into the process sufficient concern for getting the structure right. We had a lot of success with our assignments and this structure was our way of juggling all the different aspects of writing them.

Exams

The preparation for exams was not that different from the preparation for assignments. The difficulty with exams is that you are either able to handle them or not. Your preparation work may be fine but if you are not good in a timed environment, you're going to struggle in any event. I'm lucky enough to be able to keep myself in the game with exams. I'm not going to get such a poor mark that the chances of a First fly out the window.

The way we approached the exams was to try and mirror our strategy for the assignments as much as we could. Fundamentally the strategy is still the same. Like the assignments, the exams are decided by the module leader. There is still information to be obtained beforehand that will make clearer what is expected in the exam answer. It's a case of ask the right questions in the right way and at the right time. Our build up to the exams went as follows:

1 Questions about the assignment in lectures (usually at the end of class)
2 Choose topic
3 Begin literature collection
4 Questions among the other students about their approaches
5 Questions in class about our topic
6 Begin reading
7 Make preparatory notes
8 Meet with the tutor and discuss how to get a Distinction
9 Collect other students' tips and resources
10 Thorough preparation (notes, reading)

You may ask how I knew the topics that were going to be in the exam. That really was a matter of how much information the lecturers were prepared to give the class. They usually ballpark the general areas, although some are a bit mean and keep you totally in the dark. Part of it comes down to luck.

The one-to-one interviews gave us little insights that were crucial. Those interviews really did have the most impact of all the things we did during our preparations. The rest, when it comes to exams, is down to how much time you're prepared to put into it. You can't get away from working hard and that shines through in the exam mark.

Plan B is a covert operation to break into the university admin offices and photocopy the answers. If you can do it this way, I'm in. I am always drawn to the easiest option.

Basic techniques

For our exams something became obvious afterwards that we had taken for granted beforehand: exam technique. This is an absolute basic but you'd be surprised how many talented students played themselves out of the game by poor exam technique. The main point is that you need to work out beforehand how much time you have for each question and then stick to it rigidly.

We worked out that for most exams we had two questions to answer in three hours, so that's $1^1/_2$ hours for each. Where the marks are allocated unequally for questions, adjust accordingly.

You'd be surprised how many talented students played themselves out of the game by poor exam technique

There are easy marks to earn at the start of each question, which you need to pick up to get a First. It's really a matter of common sense. Lots of students gave themselves too little time to answer the later questions because they lacked the discipline to cut off the earlier answers. Their marks reflected poor answers on the later sections.

Beyond this point, concentrate on things like planning your answer, reading the question properly and so on. They are important because they are all possible pitfalls. Be aware of them. Remember: it's about keeping yourself in the game so you still have a chance.

I am not the greatest at exams but I'm certainly not the worst. I can probably claim to be able to fulfil my potential now better than most. If you're not good at exams don't sweat. For my law degree I returned some shockers (38%, 40%, 42%, 41%) so I know what its like to get bad marks. I had more than a couple of resits too. Character building/pain in the arse.

The preparation helps enormously in staying composed in the exam hall. This makes a big difference because if you're not in a state of panic you can perform better. Here's a little story. I remember reading about a study that was done years ago about samurai in Japan. It was to do with their heartbeats when they were sword fighting. I recall that the difference between the students and the grand masters was not too great with wooden swords, but when they fought with real swords the grand masters' pulses stayed close to resting. They won every time, and the study suggested that they were able to perform more effectively because they were calmer and more collected, which was reflected in the heartbeats.

If you can recreate this phenomenon in the exam room, and not be flustered, then you can improve your performance. (Don't take it too far, I'm not sure they'll allow you into the exam room in full samurai dress.)

Trick of the memory

Another key thing is that so often exams are to do with memory and not ability. I've passed loads of exams on the back of being able to remember large amounts of information over a period of

"I'll spend two hours on the first question 'cos it's quite tricky, and that will give me a clear 15 minutes for each of the essays. That should do it."

one or two days. Ask me about it a week later and I may not even remember I took the exam. Memory makes a difference and having a good memory can bump your mark up.

The best thing you can do is practise memory tricks. The best techniques are closely related to magic. A lot of magic tricks are based on memory tricks, so read up on a few basic magic tricks and you'll start to get to grips with how to improve your memory.

I tried to make sure that I could remember the important points on a few outside topics to show wider reading than just the standard texts. You're only talking brownie points here but it all helps, especially if your work is borderline (whether that's borderline First or borderline Pass).

Regardless of your particular ability at exams, I am entirely confident that the reason I did well was that I followed the strategy to prepare me well for the exams I took. This will apply to you as much as it applied to me. Don't get too concerned about the results for getting Firsts if exams aren't your thing. It's all about keeping yourself in the game. As long as you don't get a mark that's miles away from your target then the strategy will make up the remainder in your coursework.

13

Motivation

The course took a long time and it was not surprising that we lost a little of our motivation at times throughout the course. This is only natural I feel. We were aware of the various kinds of motivation theory through our sporting background and we tried to put it into play. Everyone will find it hard going at times and I think it's really a case of finding what works for you. I turned to lots of sources either to respark my enthusiasm or to keep it alive during crucial periods.

I used food (I'm a chocoholic), potential success, potential failure, snappy quotations, audio CDs, you name it. I tried loads of things to keep me motivated because without that motivation to do the work, and do it well, you can easily lose sight of the goal. It's only sensible to pay attention to how you're motivating yourself, because without it you will struggle to keep up the hard work on the days when you're not up for it.

This is time well spent. Companies spend thousands of pounds each year trying to motivate staff by sending them to conferences, seminars and the like. If you can find something that sparks you to work each day then you'll be ahead of the game. Find something that makes a difference to you. Spending a little time trying to find your muse for this particular notion will be time far better spent then reading, doing coursework or anything mundane like that.

I'll give you a couple of mine. Firstly, I'm a dreamer. One of my great motivations is a picture in my head of an immaculate white beach on a tropical island. The sky is clear blue and in the middle shines a perfect sun. I'm lying in a hammock with a cocktail in my hand without a care in the world. This is my dream life. Secretly, I long to do nothing all day and get away with it. My logic is that this isn't likely to happen unless I put the work in to get there. It always gives me a lift.

Another way I've found that works for me is to read books of quotations. Great things. A good one will cost you about a tenner and has a section of quotes for every circumstance. Here are two I like:

"A diamond is just a lump of coal that stuck to its job"
Leonardo Da Vinci

"Keep on keeping on" *Joe Dirt*

I like Leonardo's because, to me, it implies that something very ordinary can change into something exceptional by sticking at it. I like Joe Dirt's because it makes me laugh. Laughter's everything. Find something that works for you. Whatever floats your boat. It also helps if you like what you're doing in general. I didn't enjoy my law degree in that I found out after about six months that I don't like law. I call 500 lawyers at the bottom of the sea 'a good start'. This affected my motivation on that course without doubt. Consider whether you're in a similar position.

"Here's a good one: 'Hard work never killed anybody,
but why take a chance?' "

Presentation

The presentation of the essays must fit with your strategy for getting a First. It was something we felt we had an advantage with because when we saw other people's presentations they hadn't really produced much more than plain black and white documents stapled together.

We tried to brand our essays by presenting them in a similar format that we felt was professional and impressive. Essentially we were looking to create a positive impression of the essays before they'd even been opened. All essays were presented in colour with as many illustrations and figures as possible. It adds to the professional feel of the thing. We looked at the layout of the essays, how the headings should look, how the subheadings should be used to break up the work into readable pieces. We looked at everything.

We had each of our essays bound in folders with clear plastic fronts to give them an extra differentiation. We felt that having them bound hard book style would possibly give the wrong impression. We wanted to go beyond what everyone else was doing to make sure that ours were among the best presented submissions.

As a time saving factor I used the same style each time I submitted an assignment. This sort of work takes time and once you've got something you're happy with there's no reason not to use it for every essay. Each marker will be seeing it for the first time so it won't be noticed. You'll give the same good impression for each assignment with the groundwork only being done once.

Beyond that we paid a bit extra to make sure that we were using 120g, brilliant white paper so again it would stand out among the normal paper the other students would be using. Image is everything.

Presentation of *yourself* is a big deal

When it comes to exams there isn't much you can do because it's a timed environment. You differentiate yourself there by the work you've done beforehand, making sure that you've met with the module tutors and you understand what they are looking for in a Distinction class answer. The structure you use should set you apart from the rest because your preparation will have shown you what they're looking for.

"How much for a leather binding with gold tooling and
marbled endpapers?"

Personal presentation

Presentation of *yourself* is a big deal. The biggest deal. How you hold yourself in everyday life is, in my opinion, the most important factor you could ever work on. It influences everything else. Image is everything so dress well. I'm not talking black tie in workshops, but making an effort and looking tidy and clean goes a long way.

Presentation of ourselves was one of the most important factors in our success. We presented ourselves well to everybody. I've always tried to be courteous and good mannered to everybody at all times. A good morning and a firm handshake goes a long way towards creating a good impression and this never wears off. It's the same for everybody all over the world. A smile and a 'How ya doing?' is one of the most important tools in an ambitious student's box of tricks. Use it like it's going out of fashion. To everybody, all the time. More, more, more. Can't do enough of this. One thing we did that paid serious dividends was to do it to people we didn't know. Random acts of conversation do not get you known as a nutcase. It leads to people getting to know you and then being willing to help you.

15

Blagging it

I thought it would be best to give you the strategy in its entirety before I gave you the little secrets of how we applied it. By this stage I hope you've realised it's not all about bullshit, but bullshit is like the icing sugar on a cake. It sweetens the deal. At times we were in situations where we were utterly out of our depth, and our good work was seriously in danger of being flushed down the toilet.

And not on small things either. One such example is that in our first seminar people in the class started talking about a man called Henry Mintzberg. He's one of the leading authorities on business thinking in the world, and will no doubt go down in history as one of the true greats of business thinking in the same way we remember Da Vinci for art and Plato for philosophy. Not knowing who he was could be likened to being on Match of the Day saying, "Who's David Beckham?"

I hadn't a bloody clue. But for the other people in the room to take any notice of me I had to be able to argue about his theories. The answer was to look him up in my big black business book. It told me who he was, what his theories were, what the pros and cons of the arguments were, and did all this in two pages. Marvellous. Now I was armed with enough information to blag my way through the seminars until I'd seen enough of his work to fully grasp what the hell he was talking about.

It's not all about bullshit, but bullshit is like the icing sugar on a cake

Everyone will come up against this at some stage. On each course there will be some elementary points that you've never heard of before and you've got to be able to give the impression you have. It's not so much saving face as protecting your reputation.

One of the key ways I blagged my way through the early seminars and lectures (after about three months you've come across most things in the subject so it's not so necessary) was to have at least one or two things that I was well informed about in each lesson. When these topics came up, I dominated them. Get your comments in early and you've sown the seed in the lecturer's head that you're prepared. You've also sown the seed in the heads of the other students that you know what you're talking about. Then you can pipe down for the rest of the lecture. This won't be a problem because lecturers have a habit of wanting to involve the whole class and not just the talkative ones. Once you've said something they'll want to hear what someone else has to say.

This can be pushed further than you would imagine. You can give the impression that you've read a whole book by throwing in some well chosen quotes and dominating the areas they apply to. Once you've flung out a quote the other students will be terrified. This will help disguise your ignorance in the majority of the other areas of discussion. Merely giving your opinion on what other people have said will be enough to keep you involved without putting you in the spotlight.

Honourable blagging

It's important to note that this will eventually bite you back. One of the cruel parts of blagging is that eventually you run up against a brick wall and someone knocks you back. It's inevitable. I found that this challenging predicament was minimised if I restricted myself to what I call 'honourable blagging'. Such a wild misuse of terms needs explaining, I hear you cry. Quite right.

Honourable blagging is trying to mask uselessness for a brief time until you've mastered the subject you're purporting to be good at. All you're really doing is trying to hold the fort until you know enough to be legitimately at the table for open discussions. This contrasts with 'outright blagging', which is trying to mask uselessness indefinitely. Then things can really cave in if you get found out. So there you are; honourable blagging. Not to be confused with 'blagging with honours', which I'd define simply as blagging to an exceptional standard.

"Psst! Any of you guys know who this Shakespeare bloke is?"

Shift in style

Another aspect of our strategy involved a subtle difference in our behaviour when we were in different classes, tailored to suit the particular preferences of the lecturers and people in the class. We had lecturers who were more serious than others. Don't laugh as much in these people's classes because they tend to associate laughing with poor students.

And we had a few interesting situations. One lecturer, we felt, thought we didn't belong on the course. Too young. Maybe he had a point, I don't know. But we could tell he had a problem with us. So we went out of our way to try and not do anything in lectures that he could seize on as proof of his opinion. We dressed more formally for his lectures. We tried to take an interest in a few projects we knew he had on the go. We still met with him about the coursework and, although it was like getting blood from a stone, got a few helpful hints. He never fully came round but it was better than taking the other route of arguing with him.

Another lecturer seemed to be looking for relief from the boredom of long, drawn out lessons. We tried to be bright and bubbly in his classes and got everyone in the class laughing and enjoying the debates. This turned into the most enjoyable lecture for everyone and, coincidentally, seemed to have the highest attendance.

The point is an important one; each lecturer will have their own preferences which you should try to identify early on. Then spend the rest of the course fulfilling this preference. This is really more charm than blag, but it's all from the same family of mischief.

The Dissertation

The dissertation is such an important part of the overall mark that it demands lots of attention on its own. Our dissertation was worth a third of our overall mark and there is every chance that your dissertation will be equally important even if it doesn't have quite the same number of credits attached to it.

There is also every chance that whether you achieve a First or not will be greatly influenced by how you do in your dissertation. In any event it's massively important whatever your aims or expectations are. It demands special attention, which is exactly what we gave ours.

I had the experience of my law dissertation to draw upon. If you don't have such an experience don't worry because here are my mistakes in all their glory:

- I spent too little time on the whole thing; with the end result that I was forced to live the dissertation for about a month before hand in, rather than have a nice, easy run towards the deadline. The key lesson was not to keep putting it off.

- I didn't meet with my supervisor until very late, shockingly bad error really, and didn't decide on a topic until two months before the deadline. Quite an achievement given that the uni had been putting on classes for two years beforehand specifically about the dissertation.

- I had employed a policy of either not turning up or talking absolute nonsense when I eventually did. Don't do this. When people find out you've been telling them an elaborate lie for over 18 months they tend to become cross. All it really takes is a 15 minute sit down to think about what would be suitable and you're there. And my advice is make your decisions early.

For our MBA we had great difficulty in choosing topics. There's a number of important factors that must be taken into consideration and they are all tough decisions. The topic must hold academic credibility, and this usually means that you're required to justify why you think it's a contemporary (current) topic. This can be more difficult than you'd first imagine. I had several ideas refused by my supervisors and by other tutors because they'd just read an article that hadn't outlined that there were further research opportunities in those particular areas. I'd have argued otherwise but the evidence was against me and it was generally there in black and white. So bear this problem in mind. You will have an advantage if you choose your topic early and get to a stage where that topic has been approved by the people who count.

Like I say, I had several ideas knocked back and this meant that I only got going on an accepted idea fairly late on in terms of the time allocated for our dissertation. Stephen wasn't much further ahead. Other people were ahead of us, and were further ahead earlier on. If you can get ahead of the people on your course this would be to your advantage.

●

Thinking about (or starting) your dissertation early is a great way to put yourself ahead of the game

●

Because of the nature of the MBA I struggled to find time to think about the dissertation until it came to the front of my to-do list. Finding time for all our modules was tough enough quite frankly. For a first degree, where there's more time available to you, thinking about (or starting) your dissertation early is a great way to put yourself ahead of the game.

Our schedule was dictated by the sheer amount of work that we had. We had set out to use all the time available for each piece of work so the most focused time spent on each assignment was when it was the next piece of work due in. We took a one year course and this meant that we had time after all the other modules were finished which we could dedicate to the dissertation. It gave us roughly four months to complete a master's level dissertation.

This was all I had because the workload beforehand meant it had been virtually impossible to work on the dissertation without taking time away from other assignments. Much as I tried, eventually I reached this period without having had a topic or title approved. That gave me a little under four months to come up with something and get to work trying to get the First I needed to get a First overall.

Go back to your roots

During this time I had the benefit of seeing how other students were progressing with their dissertations. I paid particular attention to the problems that were common and the ways in which students were overcoming them. One of the most common problems students were complaining about was not being able to get the interviews they needed to make their studies valid. They'd chosen to look at companies and done work on them only to find that their interviewee would cancel the interview just before it was to take place. An interesting problem.

My answer to this was to consider what my area of expertise was. In my case my background is sports. I had worked with numerous sporting teams including Newcastle United and Wales RFU. All my contacts were in sport or as a direct result of sport. The way I saw it, I would be far more likely to succeed in getting an interview if I used people I knew already, or could get an introduction to using our own and our father's contacts. It worked. There were some remarkable people who agreed to be interviewed for my study who would be very difficult for other people to get to.

We both chose to do a topic that was heavily involved in sport as

"I was going to do 'Lemming migration and suicide' but I can't be
bothered to learn Lemmish."

we were confident that the people who would need to be interviewed would agree to do it because of the contacts we already had. This was a far more realistic approach than trying to rely on people who you don't know or to whom you're unlikely to receive an introduction. Stick to your background and use your contacts to get things done. Doing it straight up (e.g. from the yellow pages) will stand a high chance of failing.

Map it out

Once your topic is chosen and you've set out how you're going to go about it, you need to think about structure. The structure of your dissertation will have an enormous impact on the overall mark. Everything must fit together and the document must show consistency throughout. For this we relied heavily on research books that explain what you're supposed to be doing. To do it properly from lecture notes or your own knowledge is very difficult. We looked at what the experts said on it. They know better than I ever will so it makes sense to follow their advice strictly.

I spent as much time thinking about the best structure for my dissertation as I did about the actual content. When I say best I mean the most logical structure that will show consistency on the contents page. For example, I tried to get as much similarity as I could in the headings of the literature review chapter and the data analysis chapter so that it was very obvious why I looked at those areas in the dissertation, and where the expertise and support for my analysis came from.

The pattern of the dissertation followed the same approach as the assignments that had gone previously. We tried to find out as much about what our individual supervisors liked in their dissertations as we could. We held lots of meetings with them to get their thoughts on what they'd like to see.

●

I learnt far more from the dissertations that got Distinctions than I did from the ones that were close to my topic

●

This followed a similar line of questioning to the assignment meetings. Basically, what do I need to put in the dissertation to get a First? Then tailor the work to suit the supervisor. We also tried to establish who would be our second marker, and find out what they liked and how we could accommodate what they would want to see in the work.

The main thing about a dissertation is that it's got to show a link from the objectives in the introduction to the summary of your findings in the conclusion. They want to see you set out what you're intending to research and then give a direct response to exactly that at the end. I found out from one of my lecturers an interesting point to consider on this. He said he generally read the introduction and then flipped straight to the conclusion to see if the questions set out in the intro had been answered. What a devious side-step! This information demanded some thought. I decided directness was the answer. In the intro I used the sub-heading "Aims & Objectives" whereby I set out in plain English what I was trying to find out. In the conclusion I used the creative sub-heading "Response to Aims & Objectives". Brilliantly blunt. I'd encourage being obvious with the sub-headings in this way. Then it's easy to see that you've got a logical progression to your work.

Check out the best

The next port of call was to do some investigation into which of the dissertations that were held in the library had received Distinctions. I was lucky enough to get the names of five students who'd all got Distinction in their dissertations. For this I had a variety of sources. I started by visiting every lecturer I knew (and got on well with) and asked if they could help me out. Some did, some didn't. In addition to that I informed the other students of this ingenious plan and urged them to use the contacts they had to find out similar information.

Some came back with new names of people who'd got Distinctions and we were in business. I looked at each name and selected five that I thought I could learn the most from. These five were then photocopied in full. It took me a whole day to do but it was crucial to me getting a good mark. I then looked around for dissertations on my topic and found a few that could be useful. I often heard students being told that they should get in the library and look at dissertations on their topic for ideas. I learnt far more from the dissertations that got Distinctions than I did from the ones that were close to my topic.

Here's what I found:

- They gave me an idea of the standard that I needed to get up to.

- They showed me the structure that I should follow. They all had similar structures so I closely aligned mine with theirs.

- The level of referencing in each one was pretty similar and this made clear the level I would need to reach to better their efforts. This is always easier when you know what you're aiming at.

- They gave me insight into what the methodology should look like, because there is only a limited number of ways to explain a thing. I could closely follow what they'd written because I was using a similar methodological approach but now I had the certainty that this was what was required to get a First.

- They told me the standard of argument expected and the depth that would be required.

- They showed me the format that would be expected and how to present it in a manner that befits a distinctive dissertation.

This can be applied to anyone's dissertation effort and have an enormously positive effect. It's a question of making the goal clear. Once you know what you're competing against you can start to think about the way you're going to match it or, hopefully, better it. Year on year the standard doesn't change that much, so obtaining the past dissertations that got Distinctions should give a pretty good indication of what competition you're likely to be facing in your academic year.

The dissertation is as much about application as it is about strength of argument. It takes a lot of work. The chance that you're going to be able to get into the flow of things and write most of it in one or two sittings is very slim. It takes preparation and attention to detail. Once I had a topic that I was happy with, I planned out how I would go about the project in the early stages. I figured there was no point in putting thoughts down at this stage because I was largely uninformed on the topic in an academic sense. First port of call would be data collection.

Assemble the information

I spent a month collecting data. I downloaded as many articles as I could find and bought every book I could find on the topic. Most of this purchasing took place on amazon.co.uk because I found it to be the most productive way of searching for lots of titles on my topic in a short space of time.

I aimed to be well into my reading by the end of the month while the last few books were being delivered. I also considered the length of the reference lists and bibliographies of the Distinction dissertations I'd found, and then set a target which would give me an advantage over theirs.

The next stage was simple. Get to grips with the topic. I tried to have a good understanding of what the current thoughts were on my chosen topic. I'd read and highlighted lots of books that were similar but all argued slightly different viewpoints and would all give me something in my literature review. My supervisor had mentioned that he was of the opinion that books were likely to be more in depth than articles which would usually be making a small point. He thought there was more scope in books so that's where I directed my research.

Get down to writing

With time pressing down I started writing. It wasn't easy. I found that because I had to take consideration of so many things for each chapter I was struggling to make progress quickly. I decided to break the work down into manageable parts that I could complete in one sitting while still producing work that would be up to scratch.

Our word limit was 15,000 words. After drafting the introduction and the elementary parts of my literature review (do the easy stuff first was my motto) I found I had about 5,000 words. At this stage I had two months left with 10,000 words to go. I decided to try and complete at least 300 quality words each day for a month. That doesn't sound a lot but it takes more time than you think when you've got to make sure references are right and find references from lots of different sources.

Three hundred words per day was enough work to be making progress and was little enough that I could do it each day without burning out my enthusiasm after a few days. Also, 300 or so words a day for a month would bring me to the 15,000 word mark with a month left to spruce it up if need be. Little victories.

This worked for me largely due to my sporting background. Training every day to improve a particular aspect of your game is a gradual thing. You learn early on that you're not going to train for a week and turn into Pele or Jonny Wilkinson. It takes years to become world class and the best way to do it is to break things down into daily tasks and succeed at them each day.

This plan worked superbly well and I found 300 words easy enough to do when I'd lost patience with the project (which can and probably will happen to everyone more than once because it takes such a long time). I also used the days where I'd got into the flow of things and wrote a lot to reward myself with days off. It's too long a project not to have breaks from it. That brings me to the next stage of the plan.

Recharge your batteries

Las Vegas! We factored in a week off with a month to go until hand in to take an entire week off from even thinking about the dissertation. This helped tremendously and my God did we need the break. We were lucky enough to be able to get away abroad and when we compared prices Las Vegas, believe it or not, came up remarkably cheaply both to get there and for room rates. So why not?

The entertainment on show in Vegas provided the perfect break; I don't think I could have gone anywhere else and never thought about the dissertation. There were too many distractions to be thinking about work. Perfect! If it sounds like I've become a Vegas addict then that's because I am. I'm hooked and I admit it.

The important point here is that we factored in a week's break to recharge for the home straight. When we got back we were refreshed and ready to give it our best shot. We found that we saw the work in a new light after taking time off. There were one or two bits of restructuring and a few additions to the content to fill holes in my argument that I would have struggled to see had I not left the work alone for a while.

Taking a break gives you a more independent view, letting you see what you've actually written instead of what you *think* you've written. It's similar to when football clubs bring in a new coach for an objective view of the squad. It helps you identify players with big reputations who aren't cutting the mustard but the management has become too close to see it.

Get an independent view

We used the time right up until the hand in date to go through the work as many times as we could. Stephen, Trevor Hauser (a fellow student on our course) and I decided that two independent opinions were better than one. So we all read each other's dissertations, firstly to proof read effectively and secondly to give comment on the strength of the arguments, and improvements that could be made.

Independent views are crucial because you might not always have transferred what you want to say onto paper. They are also a great reassurance that you're on the right track if both readers give good comments. One thing I will say is that, if possible, plan for this process to take two to three days. It takes a long time to read 15,000+ words and you need to take breaks to keep focused on what you're trying to do.

Conclusion

So there it is. I hope you liked it. I've racked my brains and there really isn't an awful lot more we paid attention to. I've certainly included all the main reasons behind our success. I hope I've managed to get across that it wasn't the actual work that caused us to get the Distinctions, it was the thinking that went in before-hand.

There will certainly be ways to improve on our strategy and I hope that I've opened your mind to find them. It's a matter of how far you're prepared to go. There's some sound thinking in here (trust me) and it should help you play the game a bit more, which is just a lot easier than doing things straight up, isn't it?

Remember, the golden rule for getting a First (or avoiding a Third) is simple: Everything you do must put you in the top bracket. Cover all bases and although you might not be the outright best every time, you'll certainly stand a greatly improved chance of getting a First in the long run.

I sincerely hope that I've at least made a positive difference to your studies. If you think that it has made a difference, I'd encourage you to get into the spirit of helping others and tell friends about this book. Remember the suggestion I made in the intro though, which is that this strategy works best if the people you're applying it to (i.e. the fellow students and lecturers on your course) don't know you're doing it. Let's not go crazy. I'd not share it with too many people who could directly interfere. Other than that, tell away. Also tell parents with kids at uni (*hint, hint*). If it helps your friends get good marks, hopefully Firsts, then that can't be bad either. The more, the merrier in my opinion.

Thanks for your time.

Mark

Hear Mark talk about his strategy in person

Mark will be giving a series of seminars around the UK to pass on his tips and techniques for getting a First. If you would like to see his seminar programme, or to arrange a seminar with him, check out the details at

www.steveblack.co.uk.

Contact us

You're welcome to contact White Ladder Press if you have any questions or comments for either us or the author. Please use whichever of the following routes suits you.

Phone: 01803 813343 between 9am and 5.30pm

Email: enquiries@whiteladderpress.com

Fax: 01803 813928

Address: White Ladder Press, Great Ambrook, Near Ipplepen, Devon TQ12 5UL

Website: www.whiteladderpress.com

What can our website do for you?

If you want more information about any of our books, you'll find it at **www.whiteladderpress.com**. In particular you'll find extracts from each of our books, and reviews of those that are already published. We also run special offers on future titles if you order online before publication. And you can request a copy of our free catalogue.

Many of our books also have links pages, useful addresses and so on relevant to the subject of the book. You'll also find out a bit more about us and, if you're a writer yourself, you'll find our submission guidelines for authors. So please check us out and let us know if you have any comments, questions or suggestions.

Fancy another good read?

If you've enjoyed reading *The Insider's Guide to* **Getting a First** *(or avoiding a Third)*, how about trying another of our books? You'll find them all on our website at www.whiteladderpress.com. Meanwhile, here's a close up look at one of them.

The Voice of Tobacco *A dedicated smoker's diary of not smoking* by Richard Craze is a different kind of book about quitting. It's funny, irreverent, and resolutely refuses to preach. If you (or anyone you know) is struggling to kick the habit, this is the book for you. Here's the introduction to give you a flavour of it.

THE VOICE OF TOBACCO

INTRODUCTION

"It's 106 miles to Chicago, we've got a full tank of gas, half a pack of cigarettes, it's dark, and we're wearing sunglasses. Hit it." *Blues Brothers*

I know. I know. There's you thinking I'm not a proper smoker. I always thought the same thing. You buy a book about giving up smoking and you think this could never have been written by a proper smoker like me. Well, let's get a few things straight. Firstly, this isn't a book about *you* giving up smoking. This is a book about *me* giving up smoking. As to whether or not you give up, I couldn't give a toss. If you want to, and this helps, good. If it doesn't, well, I never said it would.

Secondly, I *am* a proper smoker. I am more a smoker than anyone else will ever be. I am more a smoker than anyone else has ever been. I am Mr Smoking Man. I drew my first delightful lung cooling wonderful drag aged six. I was caned at school for having five Weights (a brand called Weights sold in a packet containing only five cigarettes, obviously aimed directly at the under-11s' market) in my back pocket aged 10. Or rather there were only three left in the packet hence the cane for having smoked at least two of them. At 12 I was smoking 10 a day, every day. I have smoked butts from the ashtray, smoked fags down so low I have had to use a pin to hold them, and dried out fag ends that I'd put out in a can of beer. You realise, of course, that I only did this when I was out of tobacco – you have to have some pride, you know.

I have lived and breathed smoke all my adult life. I have praised its virtues and encouraged others often and willingly. I have always despised non-smokers. I have torn down no smoking signs wherever I've gone. I once seriously considered going to live in France because their attitude to smokers is so much more grown up than ours – and when I say seriously I mean seriously to the point where I was in France looking at properties.

I have got up in the night for a fag regularly for many years being unable to go the whole sleepy eight hours without one.

As I smoked each one I was already looking forward to the next. In restaurants I order what is quickest to eat not tastiest so that I can be smoking again faster. While smoking a roll-up I have been known to be rolling the next one so I can light up again immediately the one I am smoking is finished. I've been known to have two on the go at once. I have smoked throughout respiratory tract infections, flu, bronchitis, sore throats, infections, colds, viruses, illnesses and bugs. After major surgery – appendicitis etc – I have smoked immediately I came round from the general anaesthetic. I have hidden in the toilets in hospital so I could smoke while still attached to my drip.

I have smoked where it said not to, on planes, trains, buses, in stations, airports, taxis, shops, restaurants, pubs, hotels, lifts, you name it and I've smoked there. *And* at my mother's cremation, her last big puff. She died of lung cancer due to her smoking. I am Mr Smoking Man indeed.

I have smoked not only after sex but before and, when I could get away with it, during. I have smoked in the rain, in the bath, even in the shower. I have smoked while cooking, working, driving, shaving, reading, watching telly and eating. My last gasp before going to sleep was the last puff of a fag. My first gasp as I bump-started my lungs each morning was a fag before I had got out of bed, before I had opened my eyes, before the last dream had faded, before I was even conscious.

Don't tell me I'm not a proper smoker. I make ordinary smokers look like school children behind the bike sheds having their first puff. I am Mr Smoking Man. Or rather was. I am not smoking now. This is why and how.

Here's what a few of **The Voice of Tobacco**'s reviewers have had to say about it:

> It is, without doubt, the most original book on the subject of smoking – and, more pertinently, what happens when you try to stop – ever published... it is, in its own way, inspirational and undoubtedly will be the most unusual book you'll read this year. **Sunday Express**

> So many things are said in this book that we have all thought somewhere along our lung-polluted journey. However, they are not being said in the usual sanctimonious way of the pundits, doctors, vested interests or just plain killjoys. They are said honestly and with a good lung-wrenching laugh. **Inside Time**

Richard Craze is rather brave to have written such a shockingly honest book...Best of all, the book never patronises or preaches, a danger he is well aware of: 'God, I sound like a non-smoker and that was something I promised I would never do,' he writes at one point. **forestonline.org**

It's a far from easy task for Craze, as he battles against 'the voice of tobacco', a hilariously scripted idiosyncratic voice which continues to haunt him throughout. Witty and well-researched. Top stuff. **ICE magazine**

This is one man's quirky story of giving up the evil weed, written by someone who truly loves his cigs and calls himself a 'proper smoker'. Craze had his first taste of tobacco aged six, and by the age of ten he was on a pack a day. If this guy can give it up for good, anyone can. **Fresh Direction**

Why not try it out for yourself? If you'd like to order a copy of *The Voice of Tobacco* (£6.99, free p&p) you can do so via any of the routes on page 108 or using the order form at the back of this book.

The
White
Ladder
Diaries

"To start a business from scratch with a great idea but little money is a terrifying but thrilling challenge. White Ladder is a fine example of how sheer guts and drive can win the day."
TIM WATERSTONE

Have you ever dreamed of starting your own business?

Want to know what it's like? I mean, what it's really like?

Ros Jay and her partner, Richard Craze, first had the idea for White Ladder Press in the summer of 2002. This is the story of how they overcame their doubts and anxieties and brought the company to life, for only a few thousand pounds, and set it on its way to being a successful publishing company (this is its third book).

The White Ladder Diaries isn't all theory and recollections. It's a real life, day-by-day diary of all those crucial steps, naïve mistakes and emotional moments between conceiving the idea for a business and launching the first product. It records the thinking behind all the vital decisions, from choosing a logo or building a website, to sorting out a phone system or getting to grips with discounts.

What's more, the diary is littered with tips and advice for anyone else starting up a business. Whether you want to know how to register a domain name or how to write a press release, it's all in here.

If they could do it, so can you. Go on – stop dreaming.
Be your own boss.   £9.99

Recipes *for* Disaster*s*

How to turn kitchen cock-ups
into magnificent meals

**"Methinks 'twould have spared me much grief had
I had this cunning volume to hand when I burnt those
cursèd cakes."** *King Alfred the Great*

It was all going so well… friends for lunch, guests for dinner,
family for Christmas. You're planning a delicious meal, relaxed
yet sophisticated, over which everyone can chat, drink a glass of
fine wine and congratulate you on your culinary talent.

And then, just as you were starting to enjoy it – disaster! The
pastry has burnt, the pudding has collapsed or the terrine won't
turn out. Or the main ingredient has been eaten by the cat. Or
perhaps it's the guests who've buggered everything up: they
forgot to mention that they're vegetarian (you've made a beef
bourguignon). Or they've brought along a friend (you've only
made six crème brûlées).

But don't panic. There are few kitchen cock-ups that can't be
successfully salvaged if you know how. With the right attitude
you are no longer accident-prone, but adaptable. Not a panicker
but a creative, inspirational cook.
Recipes for Disasters is packed with
useful tips and ideas for making sure
that your entertaining always runs
smoothly (or at least appears to,
whatever is going on behind the scenes).
Yes, you still can have a reputation as a
culinary paragon, even if it is all bluff.

£7.99

Order form

You can order any of our books via any of the contact routes on page 108, including on our website. Or fill out the order form below and fax it or post it to us.

We'll normally send your copy out by first class post within 24 hours (but please allow five days for delivery). We don't charge postage and packing within the UK. Please add £1 per book for postage outside the UK.

Title (Mr/Mrs/Miss/Ms/Dr/Lord etc)

Name

Address

Postcode

Daytime phone number

Email

No. of copies	Title	Price	Total £
Postage and packing £1 per book (outside the UK only):			
	TOTAL:		

Please either send us a cheque made out to White Ladder Press Ltd or fill in the credit card details below.

Type of card ☐ Visa ☐ Mastercard ☐ Switch

Card number

Start date (if on card) _____ Expiry date _____ Issue no (Switch)

_____

Name as shown on card

Signature